# ARRANGING THINGS

# ARRANGING THINGS

COLIN KING

WRITTEN WITH SAM COCHRAN

RIZZOLI
NEW YORK
New York · Paris · London · Milan

*Contents*

wonderland
annie leibovitz
samu Noguchi

# *Foreword*

BY ROBIN STANDEFER

The practice of arranging has deep artistic roots—from the composition of musical notes in a symphony to the grouping of everyday items in a Dutch still life. Arrangements are ultimately about relationships, placing or juxtaposing objects to tell a story, to evoke an emotion. This intimate connection with objects has always been a meaningful part of my life, both at home and at my architectural and design practice, Roman and Williams. When my husband and business partner, Stephen Alesch, and I were designing the British Galleries at the Metropolitan Museum of Art, the curators had a term for this love affair: object lust. I see it as a shared philosophy among people who cannot rest unless they are collecting things—whether beach stones or priceless antiques—and finding harmony in their arrangement.

My treasured friend and frequent collaborator Colin King also hears the voices of objects. We are bonded in that way. He and I met soon after the unveiling of the Guild, Stephen's and my New York City store, which we launched to display our collection of design and furniture on our own terms, alongside works by a guild of artists and artisans whom we admire. Colin intuitively understood our vision of a collective gathering place for things you love, rather than things that fit perfectly together. He has since collaborated with us to develop the Guild's photographic narrative, capturing the intersections of art and life, culture and nature.

Colin calls himself a stylist, but I think of him as a master of arranging. What makes him such a master? He has a refined vision for both the two-dimensional and the three-dimensional, seeing the world as the camera lens does, recognizing when the frame sings. He possesses fierce focus, a precision between hand and eye. Moving a book one centimeter, adjusting the petals of a flower, adding a vase to a tabletop—these micro changes can transform the temperature of an image. Colin brings that alchemy to a room, with peaceful reverence for the objects and spaces.

At Roman and Williams, our work is bound by an ethos, not a style. Colin shares that philosophy, so his range is broad and only continues to grow as he collaborates with leaders in fields from design to photography to publishing. I feel very fortunate to have been a part of his journey.

When you do what we do, you need partners whose eyes you can trust. In that way, Colin has offered me a respite. By which I mean: I trust and admire him so completely that I have allowed myself to (sometimes) let go. I know that Colin can be my eyes, but also that he has the distance to elevate or contextualize things I'm too close to see. In the depths of the pandemic, Stephen and I couldn't travel to the home of our longtime friend and client Gwyneth Paltrow for the *Architectural Digest* cover shoot. But with Colin on set, we were confident that our work would be beautifully translated.

As a designer, you often get only one chance to document a room. That photo has to count. Colin captures a room as it ought to be remembered, pulling out the beauty and the essence of a space. This book is a meditation on the ineffable sensitivity and sophistication it takes to master that mix, on set and in real life. Colin is a deft practitioner, yes, but he is also a generous teacher, introducing others to the philosophy of object lust.



*(Page 5)* In my Tribeca living area, objects mingle on the travertine table that served as a stage for my *Stay Home Still Life* series.

*(Opposite)* A dining vignette featuring Roman and Williams furniture. Styled for Roman and Williams Guild.

# *Introduction*

## STYLING IS A DAILY PRACTICE

Any object can be a thing of beauty. Once, when styling a Manhattan apartment, I needed to complete a bedside vignette. I made do with what I could find, grabbing a pepper mill from the kitchen, flipping it on its head, and repurposing it as a vase for a stem of flowers. The lines, the scale, the silhouette—that piece made the image, but also transcended photographic form. In person, it was truly a delight to behold.

For most of us, on most days, it's easy to lose our sense of wonder. We rarely let ourselves look at objects long enough to see beyond their intended use. Styling is all about noticing the little things. It's about being decisive in the moment while giving yourself permission to change your mind. And it's about trying new arrangements again and again—finding out what the moment isn't, until you find out what the moment is. There's always the element of chance. In that regard, styling is a metaphor for life.

I'm often asked how I got where I am. In all truth, being a stylist wasn't always a career that seemed real, let alone possible. Only when the artist Jack Ceglic, whom I had met through a mutual friend, entrusted me to produce a story on his Manhattan home did I realize it was a path to pursue. I'll always remember the moment Tom Delavan, the design editor at *T* magazine, responded to my pitch, which I had emailed to the company's legal department in my naivete. (Tom ultimately passed on Jack's city apartment but said yes to his East Hampton house, published in 2019.) And I'll never forget when, some time later, Michael Shome, the visuals director at *Architectural Digest* (*AD*), contacted me to style a Marcel Breuer–designed house in Litchfield County, Connecticut—my first of countless shoots for the magazine, which now include the homes of Drake, Kirsten Dunst, Gwyneth Paltrow, Nate Berkus, and Kerry Washington. My professional journey has been one of borrowed confidence, lucky breaks, and always saying yes.

Just walk through the fear, I tell people.



*(Opposite)* At home in Tribeca.

# *Arranging Things*

## ORIGINS

Although I never set out to be a stylist, there were clues as to my destiny. Growing up in central Ohio, I spent hours collecting rocks on my family's farm—smashing them open hoping to find geodes, then lining up the fragments on my bedroom windowsill. I always went for the really ugly ones, convinced they might contain the hidden gems. They never did, but they gave me an enduring interest in the mystical power of objects, and a love for the otherwise overlooked and forgotten. Everywhere I went I picked up scraps—a piece of broken piñata, a swatch of fabric. There was energy, I discovered, in the discarded. And when, at nine, I was given a camera by my parents, I started taking pictures of my treasures, composing still lifes in my bedroom. To this day I still communicate with images.

As a kid, I was afraid of everything and everybody but somehow always found a way to be on stage. I came to dance at the age of thirteen, after a growth spurt ended my budding—let's face it, doomed—gymnastics career. Back then, I was looking for ways to be seen without speaking, afraid that my voice would out me to my Ohio peers at an all-boys Catholic school. (I was lucky to have my twin brother, Caleb, as my protector.) Dance taught me, a kid in the early stages of finding himself, a kid who didn't even know being openly gay was possible, how to study other people and blend in. But it also taught me how to move through space, creating lines and compositions. It taught me refinement. And it taught me how to express myself without words.

The life of a dancer, I would learn, can be brutal. At eighteen, I moved to New York to study at Marymount Manhattan College, falling instantly in love with the city. I went to every museum and performance and party I could. But nonstop classes and hours of scrutiny in front of a mirror took their toll, fanning the flames of insecurity while igniting an insatiable desire to make something of myself. My grandiosity collided with my wavering self-esteem. At auditions, I would look to my left and to my right and know other people wanted it more. (The life of a starving artist never appealed to me.) My parents encouraged me to find a backup career.

Restless ambition nonetheless led me to Los Angeles, where I didn't know a soul. I was twenty-two and bold. As a dancer, it was shockingly easy to get an agent. Eventually, no after no after no after no beat me down, and I traded dance for personal training, working under fitness legend Tracy Anderson. Then one day I got the call to join my private client Gwyneth Paltrow in London. I gladly tagged along, training her, Victoria Beckham, and Stella McCartney back-to-back most mornings. To be in their homes—seeing the demands placed on them, being a small part of their daily routines—was fun and inspiring. That period of my life taught me a great deal about trust and showing up for other people. Off the clock, however, I was lonely.

Upon returning to Los Angeles, my self-doubts masked by ego, life eventually got overwhelming. I felt out of control, so much so that I knew I had to make a change: I quit drinking. By the time this book comes out, I will be more than six years sober. I bring this up because recovery has become a bedrock of my worldview, instilling in me a keen awareness of life's messy undertones and a deep gratitude for every passing moment. My approach to styling builds off both, embracing the ephemeral, the bruised, and the imperfect. After trying to be perfect for so long, I learned to accept life on its own terms.

# *Introduction*

## CRAFT

So you could say my career has been a journey, not a linear one but a series of meandering circles. There were other stops and chance encounters along the way. In L.A., while working as a social media manager for a small design firm, I met the photographer Reid Rolls, who let me volunteer when he shot the Greenwich Village home of Warby Parker cofounder Neil Blumenthal. (That film would ultimately appear as an *AD* digital home tour.) In New York, after I met Tom Delavan through that first *T* magazine story, he hired me at his interior design firm, where I learned the ropes of decorating. And it was an *AD* subject, my now-dear friend Athena Calderone, who introduced me to my design heroes Robin Standefer and Stephen Alesch, for whom I helped develop the photographic narrative for Roman and Williams Guild. I may not have had a plan, but I knew when something was working—and when to move on. I just leapt into every adventure with as much grace as I could muster.

Another question I sometimes get is what exactly does a stylist do? It's not about creating a space or object from scratch. That's the purview of the designer. I have been fortunate, however, to enjoy a master class in design through my work, and now wear that hat to conceive interiors and furnishings. Nor is styling about documenting a room. That's the domain of expert photographers like my regular collaborators Adrian Gaut, Stephen Kent Johnson, William Jess Laird, and Rich Stapleton. Rather, my role as stylist is to tease out the essence of a space—to take everything in and determine how best to translate that spirit to the image. I try to call attention to undiscovered possibilities and create renewed harmony of forms without pulling focus from the room as a whole.

Every job is different. It can call for a light touch, just bringing in branches and flowers, or it can involve propping an entire house, with a week of full-blown shopping. No matter the scope of the assignment, my process is highly intuitive, informed by a loose outline but guided by forces beyond my control. I wish I had a secret I could let you in on, some sort of formula, but no such thing exists. I add or take away until the composition feels complete. That's the moment.

## STILL LIFES

In my own life, it's been a struggle to appreciate those moments. Prior to March 2020, it is no exaggeration to say I had rarely ever seen daylight in my Brooklyn Heights apartment. Mornings began before dawn, with training sessions or trips to the flower market in advance of photo shoots. Nights were a blur of dinners, openings, and events as I immersed myself in the New York design scene. But the pandemic interrupted that hustle, confining me to two rooms—four if you count my tiny galley kitchen and bath.

Desperate for a creative outlet under quarantine, I started creating a new still life each day, shopping my home and arranging whatever I had on hand into groupings and posting the results on Instagram. Loaves of bread, balanced against one another, assumed unexpected sculptural dimensions. A glass of milk, juxtaposed with a

ceramic lamp, seemed to subvert the physical properties of liquids and solids. And a single candle, documented at various stages of burning, offered a poetic reminder of time's fleeting nature. There were always opportunities to see things differently, as eggshells, pears, branches, and books revealed unexpected magic. That's what I love about styling. It's about giving reverence to ordinary items and bringing joy into your surroundings.

That routine helped keep me sane. And not just me. Over the course of the pandemic, as I expanded my photo series under the hashtag #stayhomestilllife, my Instagram following grew from seventy thousand to more than two hundred thousand. People all over the globe took up my ritual, composing their own impromptu arrangements with whatever was laying around. It gave me confidence to know that my simple pleasure also gave other people a sense of calm. Styling, I was reminded by their work, can be a daily practice, one that empowers you to see the world differently and find new meaning in your surroundings.

## KNOWLEDGE DISTILLED

While working on this book, I settled into a new apartment, a light-filled Tribeca loft that doubles as my studio. Bit by bit, I took it back to its raw state—stripping the floors, removing doors and window treatments. Walls finished in plaster by Kamp Studios now offer a muted backdrop to furnishings and objects that reflect the friendships I have made through work. There's a pedestal by Josh Greene, a stool by Green River Project, and a sofa made by the upholsterer recommended to me by Monique Gibson. My childhood self would be happy to see there are rocks in the form of my coffee table, the base of which consists of large, cleaved stones. I still believe in the mystical power of objects.

Here, in this loft, I've sifted through my portfolio, pinning photos from past projects onto moodboards, observing as themes emerged. To demystify the act of styling, each of the chapters in this book explores a new way of looking, whether meditating on positive and negative space or mining unused corners of a room. To further translate these concepts, I've organized special photo shoots, including some at my current home. I hope the results help others to distill what's important in their surroundings, to create space for beauty, and to evolve their own eye. Styling can be a tool not only to make the most of what you have, but to reconnect with the world—and with yourself. Just trust your instincts.



*(Opposite)* In my living area, the coffee table I designed—using reclaimed wood and stacks of rocks—displays piles of books in oatmeal hues.

# 1

# PARAMETERS

ACCEPTING CONSTRAINTS
TO DISCOVER NEW OPPORTUNITIES

If I've learned anything from styling, it's been to relinquish the fantasy of a blank canvas. In design, as in life, you must always navigate a series of constraints—from the proportions of a room to the dimensions of a surface to existing architectural details. Only by leaning into such challenges can you delight in the world as it is. On the job, I typically experience a space for the first time the day of the photo shoot. And by removing whatever is on display, I can immediately grasp the underlying framework. An empty shelf becomes a game of Tetris, wherein stacks of books act as building blocks. A cleared coffee table, meanwhile, reveals a grid on which to arrange items, experimenting with height. My mind automatically dissects an interior into planes. That's when you begin the process of trial and error: placing pieces instinctively, seeing where things fall. It can be overwhelming, but styling is about taking one step at a time—corner by corner, surface by surface—and trusting you'll get to the end. And the end might surprise you. When I first moved into my Tribeca loft, I hated all the beadboard and seriously considered ripping it all out. Repainted, it is now one of my favorite elements in the home. You don't need to have a plan, but you do need to understand the parameters. Nothing exists in a vacuum.

*Parameters*

(*Page 17*) At Seventh House, a vintage and contemporary design gallery in Hollywood, the curved headboard of a Green River Project bed cradles a lamp. Styled for *Ark Journal*.

(*Opposite*) A corner niche hugs my Interconnect candleholder for Menu.

(*Above*) Every opening is a frame to fill. Interior design by Axel Vervoordt for the Greenwich Hotel in New York City. Styled for Beni.

*(Above)* In a Gramercy Park town house, a floor-to-ceiling window becomes a backdrop for twin chairs. Architecture by O'Neill Rose Architects. Styled for *Rum*.

*(Opposite)* A Nolita hallway creates a vantage point to emphasize. Styled for Roman and Williams Guild.

The context of and relationship between objects are just as interesting as individual pieces. Take architecture into account—a disregarded corner, the dimensions of a windowsill, the procession of a hallway. This is your framework. Let what is there inform what you are doing.



*(Opposite)* In my Tribeca kitchen, open shelves flank the range hood, and a shallow ledge runs along the countertop—all dynamic opportunities for the arrangement of objects. Even the back of the stovetop can be used as a display area.

*(Above)* The constraints could not be clearer in the case of this Pierre Jeanneret aluminum bookcase. Styled for *Rum*.

*(Above)* A snug space can be a great fit for objects that hold their own. Styled for Zara Home.

*(Overleaf)* At the Brooklyn studio of Simone Bodmer-Turner, amorphous built-ins shelter various treasures, among them her own vessels. Styled for Simone Bodmer-Turner.

*(Above)* A bookcase needn't call for books; here, I grouped objects in like materials and complementary finishes. Styled for Zara Home.

*(Opposite)* The natural grain of this freestanding, olive-wood cabinet is a jumping-off point for ceramics in this Tribeca home. Styled for Bespoke Interiors.

*(Opposite)* Off-center, a pair of vases—one small, the other tiny—adds a refined note to a minimalist fireplace. Styled for Anthropologie.

*(Above)* An ornate mantelpiece invites busier groupings, while wall molding maps the way for art. Interior design by Max Zinser and Julian Louie. Styled for *Architectural Digest*.

*(Right)* In my Brooklyn Heights apartment, rectilinear forms complement the hearth's clean lines.

*(Overleaf)* A single open shelf provides a platform for everyday dishware and a grouping of pears—one of my styling signatures. Styled for Zara Home.

Coffee tables are one of the larger surfaces in a room. Use objects that have shape and heft to them. Play with scale, height, depth, and form. Break perpendicular and parallel lines. No two combinations are the same.

*(Opposite)* Low stacks of books in a loosely cruciform arrangement play off the dimensions of a circular coffee table. Styled for Anthropologie.

*(Above)* Objects and books create quadrants atop a square coffee table by Athena Calderone. Styled for Crate & Barrel.

*(Above)* The doorway to my Brooklyn Heights bedroom acts as a foundation to this multitiered vignette.

*(Opposite)* Furniture and art bring further focus to the statement fireplace at this Manhattan apartment. Interior design by Monique Gibson. Architecture by Ike Kligerman Barkley. Styled for *Architectural Digest*.

*(Opposite)* Incorporated into the stone backsplash, a shallow shelf forms a horizontal midline to objects above and below. Styled for Zara Home.

*(Above)* In a Manhattan apartment, shelves become stages for eclectic but similarly scaled objects. Interior design by Studio Giancarlo Valle. Styled for *Architectural Digest*.

Styling is like conquering a thousand-piece jigsaw puzzle. Start with the borders, then work in some obvious pieces. Maybe walk away and come back with fresh eyes. Eventually you get to a place where no other configuration could work.



*(Opposite)* A Minjae Kim bench and a Cory Arcangel artwork play off the curved central staircase of a Manhattan town house. Interior design by Studio Giancarlo Valle. Styled for *Architectural Digest*.

# 2

# OBJECTS IN DIALOGUE

## CREATING CONNECTIONS AND INTRIGUE THROUGH JUXTAPOSITIONS

The most compelling spaces, in my experience, are case studies in relationships. A great room not only foregrounds the unexpected connections that exist between objects, but also catalyzes new ones between those objects and ourselves. And a large part of my role as a stylist is forging those relationships, achieving clarity and meaning through the arrangement of pieces. No matter the context, I immediately take inventory of what's already around me, opening cabinets and identifying chances for subtlety and complexity . . . bringing forgotten keepsakes out while putting others away . . . varying their positions.

Where can I discover new beauty? How can I elevate the mundane? Narratives enter my head as I assign objects the roles of protagonist and antagonist (in the case of oppositional qualities) or protagonist and sidekick. Sometimes an object can't quite stand on its own. Sometimes an object needs a friend. (Don't we all!) It can come down to scale, so I vary or group pieces according to height. Or it can come down to silhouette: the convex curve of one treasure echoing the concave curve of another, something horizontal reinvigorating something vertical. Materiality, proportion, and finish all too inform my choices. I'll experiment with different arrangements until I find the juxtapositions that seem like they shouldn't make sense, yet somehow work perfectly, hanging together in restrained balance. Just allow yourself opportunities for serendipity. Those are my favorite conversations.

*(Page 45)* A medley of pieces chats it up, revealing the marks of their makers. Styled for Roman and Williams Guild.

*(Opposite)* A Giancarlo Valle side chair with a velvet-upholstered seat, a white-onyx table, and an oak screen from Studio Oliver Gustav mingle in Manhattan. Interior design by Studio Giancarlo Valle. Styled for *Architectural Digest*.

*(Above)* The rounded forms of terra-cotta vessels converse with glossy eggplants. Styled for Zara Home.

*(Overleaf)* At my Tribeca apartment, wide-ranging furnishings share a common ethos.

JB BLUNK

*(Above)* A symphony of silhouettes in an Upper East Side vignette. Interior design by Studio Mellone. Styled for *Architectural Digest*.

*(Opposite)* Objects call out to each other from across a room. Interior design by Studio Mellone. Styled for *Architectural Digest*.

Every day I look at what's around me and find new ways to play. Move things around. Ask yourself: Is this strong enough on its own, or does it need a friend? It's all about trial and error. There is no universal manual.

*(Opposite)* Three friends enjoy a mantel-top moment. Styled for Beni.

*(Above)* Curves converge in this array of designs by Athena Calderone. Styled for Crate & Barrel.

# *Objects in Dialogue*



*(Opposite)* Set on a vintage gateleg table in my Tribeca loft, a found stone holds its own in the company of patinated vessels and a stone lamp.

*(Opposite)* In this image from my *Stay Home Still Life* series, pieces by Roman and Williams Guild form a muted tableau on my travertine table, a laboratory of sorts for off-hours arranging.

*(Above)* A timeworn pocket door calls out to a fragile vessel that is displayed atop its own crate. Styled for Beni.

Don't get stuck seeing objects just for their intended use. There is wisdom to be found from loosening the rules. Lean into uncertainty.



*(Opposite)* At my Tribeca loft, a grouping of small treasures includes a Gae Aulenti table lamp from Dobrinka Salzman Gallery in Manhattan and the Converge bookends and Sentiment paperweight from my collection for Menu.

*(Opposite)* A variety of textures, revealed through subtle surfaces, adds depth to a living room grouping. Styled for Roman and Williams Guild.

*(Above)* Household staples form a balancing act in a snapshot from my *Stay Home Still Life* series.

*(Overleaf)* At the Williamsburg home of MDFG gallery cofounders Jeffrey Gratsch and Ashley Booth Klein, a gathering of vintage finds, among them pieces by Isamu Noguchi, Charlotte Perriand, and Jean Prouvé. Styled for *Rum*.

ROY DeCARAVA LIGHT BREAK

*(Opposite)* Refined vessels draw the eye across a Greenwich Village living room. Styled for Sandra Weingort.

*(Above)* Eclectic finds in an impeccably packed Manhattan corner. Interior design by Sebastian Zuchowicki. Styled for *Architectural Digest*.

Styling is not just about objects; it's about defining the space that surrounds them—pushing boundaries and creating tension to heighten our appreciation of an overall composition.

*(Above)* Diverse materials and assorted geometries achieve a cohesive composition. Styled for Roman and Williams Guild.

*(Opposite)* A study in silhouettes. Styled for Anthropologie.

*(Opposite)* A sense of movement courses through a Manhattan breakfast area. Interior design by Monique Gibson. Architecture by Ike Kligerman Barkley. Styled for *Architectural Digest*.

*(Above)* Two complementary vessels share an aside at the Simple Feast test kitchen in Oxnard, California. Styled for *Rum*.

*(Overleaf)* Placed at different angles, a collection of chairs stagger through my Brooklyn Heights apartment. Styled for *T* magazine.

AMERICAN FASHION
FRANK
THE TOUCH

MARC DU PLANTIER
CHARLOTTE PERRIAND
JOSEF FISCHNALLER · PRÄCHTIG

*(Opposite)* A confluence of curves in tonal harmony lets materials shine. Styled for Roman and Williams Guild.

# 3

# THE ART OF EMPTINESS

## CULTIVATING STILLNESS AND HONING NEGATIVE SPACE

We often feel compelled to fill the void. In conversation, it's a struggle to endure the awkwardness of a pause. We rush to break the silence, even if we have nothing to say. And the same is true of styling. The discomfort of a blank wall or surface is hard to endure. But emptiness can be an expression of potential, and a form of beauty. Dance taught me that. On stage, you must stay attuned to the vacuum around you, to the weight of those volumes. It's when the lines of your limbs interrupt those voids—when movement slices through the stillness—that magic happens. I've applied those lessons to arranging objects, eliminating excess and distilling compositions to their essence. A candleholder can look so elegant on its own. A single painting, offset, can leave a stretch of wall as a reprieve for the eye. And a coffee table can be a sculpture unto itself. Not every corner or surface needs something. I edit, edit, edit, and edit some more, stripping away the noise to communicate the most through an economy of visual language. Collecting, after all, isn't about amassing the most stuff. It's about refining. I've never regretted not filling a space.

*(Page 77)* Unfilled shelves signal new opportunities at Seventh House. Styled for *Ark Journal*.

*(Opposite)* A single task lamp sits atop an otherwise unadorned bedside table at the Greenwich Hotel. Interior design by Axel Vervoordt. Styled for Beni.

*(Above)* A low-slung sofa and Rick Owens's Stag T stool anchor a blank expanse of wall at the Brooklyn home of Mikkel Gregers Jensen. Styled for *Rum*.

Leave space to breathe. Every corner doesn't need something. Quieter moments can do a better job of drawing your eye to what's there. It's important to know when to let things be.

*(Above)* No books, no table lamp—just a water glass and pitcher beside the bed. Styled for Zara Home.

*(Opposite)* Unfurnished, a room at Palazzo Daniele in Puglia offers a poetic backdrop for one gorgeous rug. Styled for Beni.

*(Opposite)* No interventions other than natural light are needed in this sublime Marfa staircase, where a sculpture by Tony Feher is suspended from the ceiling. Architecture by Selldorf Architects. Styled for *Architectural Digest*.

*(Above)* At Seventh House, my contemporary interpretation of a monastic Dutch still life: just one chair and my Interconnect candleholder. Styled for Menu.

*(Overleaf)* At a Greenwich Village apartment, a rhapsody in white. Styled for Nicolas Schuybroek Architects.

Rosemarie Trockel A Cosmos
Outliers and American Vanguard Art

*(Opposite)* A pear balances against a rustic glass from Studio Oliver Gustav in a snapshot from my *Stay Home Still Life* series.

*(Above)* A stark view of my installation with Belgian designer Jos Devriendt at the Manhattan design gallery Demisch Danant.

*(Overleaf)* Nothing above the sofa and just a single plant on the coffee table of this conversation space at Seventh House. Styled for *Ark Journal*.

*(Above)* Only the essentials in this refined grouping at Palazzo Daniele. Styled for Beni.

*(Opposite)* Ancora, part of my Spoken Lines rug collection, grounds a sparsely furnished bedroom at Palazzo Daniele. Styled for Beni.

*(Overleaf)* A glass vase far to one side counters the asymmetry of this minimalist fireplace surround in a Gramercy Park town house. Architecture by O'Neill Rose Architects. Styled for *Rum*.

Life is a series of voids and vacuums and pauses. Eliminate the noise and sit with the truth. There's beauty in stillness.

*(Right)* My Interconnect candleholder, standing solo on a circular table by Green River Project, at Seventh House. Styled for Menu.

*(Opposite)* An undressed window frames a sylvan view of the Hudson Valley. Interior design by Post Company. Styled for Inness.

*(Above)* This hotel suite is an exercise in casual control. Interior design by Post Company. Styled for Inness.

Collecting is not about more, more, more. It's the process of refining. It's about telling a powerful story through an economy of visual language.



*(Opposite)* An impromptu arrangement of branches in a simple vessel is all this space needs. Styled for Zara Home.

4

# NATURAL POISE

## GIVING NEW LIFE TO BRANCHES, BLOOMS, AND OTHER WONDERS OF THE EARTH

I have always been inspired by the asymmetries and impermanence of nature. In the landscape, nothing is perfect and nothing is forever. Flowers wilt. Trees fall. Shores erode. Nature reminds me to embrace life's messiness, and of my tiny place in this vast universe. Nature, put simply, humbles me. As a child collecting rocks in rural Ohio, I developed a deep appreciation for the beauty of found objects: the languid gesture of a stem or the wildness of a tumbleweed. How could one ever improve upon that? So as a stylist, natural ephemera has been a lifeline. There have been times when I'll walk into a home and find there are no books or objects to display, or I arrive at the flower market too late to grab anything good. But in a pinch, mother nature delivers. I'll venture out into a garden or roam the city streets, trimming plantings (with permission) and picking up errant treasures off the ground. It's a strategy born of lack, but it's a strategy that works wonders. A stone can become a monolithic sculpture. A branch can fill a vertical void like a line drawing in space. It's all about giving reverence to ordinary objects and seeing things differently through the power of context and composition. Homeowners sometimes ask where I found something, to which I reply: "In your yard." I'll always be that farm boy in the fields.

Nothing in nature is totally linear or symmetrical. Nothing is immune to decay. That humbles me and reminds me to abandon perfection. Beauty lies in organic flaws.

*(Page 103)* An ordinary branch injects a moment of extraordinary beauty. Styled for Zara Home.

*(Above)* A wild bit of West Texas bends toward the minimalist Marfa hearth. Interior design by Jeffrey Bilhuber and Madison Cox. Architecture by Selldorf Architects. Styled for *Architectural Digest*.

*(Opposite)* Leaves of varying appearance tie together a vignette's woodland tones. Styled for Anna Karlin.

*(Overleaf)* Creeping vines and stacked stones lend mystery to the garden of Seventh House. Styled for *Ark Journal*.

*(Opposite)* At the Greenwich Hotel, a long languid branch tests the limits of balance. Interior design by Axel Vervoordt. Styled for Beni.

*(Above)* At an apartment overlooking Washington Square Park: one flower is all the bedside needs. Interior design by Ashe Leandro.

*(Overleaf)* A backyard discovery adds whimsy to a still life. Styled for Roman and Williams Guild.

*(Opposite)* A raucous arrangement of branches stands tall in a high-ceilinged Malibu kitchen. Styled for Alexander Design.

*(Above)* An overstuffed vase brings an organic touch to a Malibu living room. Styled for Alexander Design.

# *Natural Poise*

I am drawn to wildness—nothing upright or pristine but things that are languid or reaching or fragile or off-kilter. I look for the same grace in found ephemera that I discovered with dance. Maybe it's a tumbleweed. Maybe it's a vase bursting with one type of flower. We can never improve upon what's already in nature.



*(Opposite)* A foraged bough lends accumulated wisdom and beauty to my Tribeca apartment.

Paul Klee
A VISION SHARED
MID-CENTURY MODERN

*(Opposite)* In a Washington Square Park residence, a hauntingly beautiful bouquet has yet to bloom. Interior design by Ashe Leandro.

*(Above)* A sinuous branch assumes a sculptural presence in a minimalist bathroom. Styled for Zara Home.

*(Right)* Wild clippings give tension to the clean lines of Jack Ceglic's East Hampton house. Styled for *T* magazine.

*(Opposite)* Placed in a Casey Zablocki stone vase from Roman and Williams Guild, berried branches add a witchy note. Styled for Bespoke Interior Design.

*(Above)* Fuzzy and slightly bizarre flowers look pleasingly perverse in an elegant, fluted vase. Interior design by Studio Mellone. Styled for *Architectural Digest*.

*(Above and Opposite)* Simple arrangements in the spirit of ikebana accentuate sculptural vessels. Styled for Simone Bodmer-Turner.

With flowers you are at the mercy of the seasons. Surrender instead to what is available at the market or in your backyard. It might not be the perfect branch—maybe part of it looks frail—but it's about balance.



*(Opposite)* A single stem adds an unexpected perpendicular angle to a grouping of objects. Styled for Roman and Williams Guild.

# 5

# FROM THE SHADOWS

FINDING HONESTY AND MEANING IN LIGHT, DARKNESS, AND THE PASSAGE OF THE SUN

People sometimes tease that I live my life in the shadows. They're not wrong. In finished images, my work tends toward dark and moody. Just don't mistake that for melancholic contrivance. The word I use is real. I love lighting that captures the happy accidents of time and place, impacted by season, sun, and skies. And I love lighting that adds depth to objects, bringing texture and three-dimensionality—even imperfections—into focus. The dancer in me always wants to move through space, shattering flat planes. That's the power of natural light. Hour to hour, the sun's rays migrate across a room, framing objects and casting long shadows and streaks across walls, sometimes relegating entire corners to darkness. In this way, light and shadow become objects themselves, players in a larger composition. I've experienced it firsthand at home, where I've eschewed curtains and blinds altogether. The soft glow of dawn gives way to the even intensity of noon and eventually the sideways glare of sunset. It's the ultimate theater. I realize, of course, lighting must also be functional. I'll place a lamp on a coffee table or kitchen countertop. A pendant overhead can create a heightened sense of drama. Even a single candlestick can set the mood. It's all about finding those magic moments, knowing when to foreground light—and when to obstruct it.

*(Page 127)* Sun streaks across a Fort Greene stairwell. Styled for West Elm.

*(Opposite)* Diagonal shadows wash over a tabletop vignette. Styled for Roman and Williams Guild.

*(Above)* The faintest glow, emanating from the windows onto a large-scale vessel by Akiko Hirai. Styled for Roman and Williams Guild Gallery.

Where does drama invade? Where does drama recede? Even the smallest shift in lighting can be profound.

*(Above)* A trio of Jos Devriendt lamps as part of my *Passage* installation, conceived in collaboration with Demisch Danant.

*(Opposite)* Foliage shadows magnified across a blank wall. Styled for Anthropologie.

*(Opposite)* Displayed on a windowsill, curvaceous vases capture ombré effects. Styled for Zara Home.

*(Above)* Light bounces off a black-finished table, accentuating the silhouettes of various objects. Styled for *Departures*.

*(Opposite)* Glass panes create a luminous grid across the floor of a Sag Harbor bedroom. Styled for Anna Karlin.

*(Above)* Sun streams through undressed windows in Sag Harbor. Styled for Anna Karlin.

*(Above)* Three-dimensional forms emerge from the veil of darkness. Styled for Anna Karlin.

*(Opposite)* Two vessels in contrasting glazes and sizes echo light and shadow. Styled for Roman and Williams Guild.

*(Above)* An extinguished candle suggests a former flame at Vipp Studio NYC in Tribeca. Styled for *WSJ. Magazine*.

*(Opposite)* Two light fixtures converse bedside at my Brooklyn Heights apartment. Styled for *T* magazine.

Natural light is dynamic and fleeting—changing minute to minute and season to season. It can become its own object as sunlight or shadow moves across a room. And it can frame the pieces you treasure.

*(Opposite)* A diffuse glow bathes a kitchen's subtle surfaces. Styled for Anthropologie.

*(Above)* A low sun teases out a room's subtle palette. Styled for Anthropologie.

*(Right)* Raking light brings tableware textures into strong relief. Styled for Anthropologie.

*(Above)* Umbral intrigue moves across a spare place setting. Styled for Roman and Williams Guild.

*(Opposite)* Every wrinkle of fabric in focus. Styled for Anna Karlin.

*(Overleaf)* Jos Devriendt lamps release downward pools of light at my *Passage* installation for Demisch Danant.

PT-1647
HT

*(Above)* Dappled light acts as a diaphanous veil at the Greenwich Hotel. Interior design by Axel Vervoordt. Styled for Beni.

*(Above)* Shadow lends a grid to a carpet's warp and weft. Styled for Beni.

Light gives space depth, adding dimension that cannot be re-created. Leave the windows uncovered and do away with harsh overhead fixtures. A few table and floor lamps can spread the glow and draw the eye around the room.



*(Opposite)* A door ajar ushers in a runway of sun. Styled for Beni.

# 6

# VIVID DETAILS

## EMBRACING PALETTE AS POSSIBILITY AND COLOR AS OBJECT

The use of color is not something that comes naturally to me. Friends and colleagues often joke that I dream in fifty shades of brown. At home I surround myself with a medley of neutral hues, from the natural tones of various woods to notes of bone, umber, sepia, and sand. What saturated splashes of paint I do use are dark and moody—the chocolate of my Tribeca bathroom, for instance, or the deep khaki of my Brooklyn Heights bedroom. In erring on the side of beige, however, I like to think that I am holding space for color and possibility. And there is color to be found everywhere, whether in the bruised skin of ripened fruit or the verdigris of patinated metal. Styling is about identifying and romancing those subtle variations, introducing layers through glazes or textiles or blooms. On the job, of course, I encounter every possible shade of the rainbow, as deftly deployed by today's top designers. No matter the setting, I treat color like any object—looking for commonalities and differences between it and other elements of a room, playing with that tension. If a room or bookshelf is painted, I find ways to reveal that color through complementary arrangements of objects. When designing rugs for Beni, I approached the palette as I would a vignette, nailing down a foundational hue then building off it, block by block. There's always the opportunity to introduce more color, especially in a neutral space. Sometimes it just takes a breath to make up your mind.

*(Page 153)* Moroccan tiles hum in a Marfa bathroom. Interior design by Jeffrey Bilhuber and Madison Cox. Architecture by Selldorf Architects. Styled for *Architectural Digest*.

*(Above)* A quilted blue coverlet, sun-kissed wood, and multihued books harmonize in a bedroom. Styled for Hay.

*(Opposite)* A graphic Jonas Wood artwork pops at the Williamsburg home of MDFG gallery cofounders Jeffrey Graetsch and Ashley Booth Klein. Styled for *Rum*.

CS/CUB.208

*(Opposite)* Painted walls conjure an inky sky in the Manhattan apartment of Ariel Ashe. Interior design by Ashe Leandro. Styled for *Rum*.

*(Above)* At a Tribeca apartment, a shock of pink stands apart. Styled for Sandra Weingort.

Color can be an object unto itself. Treat vibrant elements not simply as pops or as backdrops but as building blocks that relate to the overall composition.

*(Above)* A bright chair in an otherwise muted apartment. Styled for Anna Karlin.

*(Opposite)* Mounted to the wall of a Manhattan apartment, a rust-colored swath of fabric complements the mustard carpet. Interior design by Studio Giancarlo Valle.

*(Overleaf)* Ocher details accent a midnight-blue bedroom in Manhattan. Interior design by Studio Giancarlo Valle. Styled for *Architectural Digest*.

la lune
est
le miroir
du temps

*(Above)* A predominately green Manhattan dining room calls for neutral objects. Interior design by Studio Giancarlo Valle. Styled for *Architectural Digest*.

*(Opposite)* Earthy browns balance the pistachio-colored walls of this Rockaway Beach bedroom. Interior design by Green River Project. Styled for *Architectural Digest*.

*(Overleaf)* Furnishings in shades of coffee, caramel, and chocolate sing in this mustard Rockaway Beach living room. Interior design by Green River Project. Styled for *Architectural Digest*.

*(Opposite)* Set against a polka-dotted golden carpet, a coffee table's crimson velvet base and ceramic top make for a bold study in contrasts. Interior design by Studio Giancarlo Valle.

*(Above)* A red-and-yellow dialogue unfolds in an assortment of tableware. Styled for Zara Home.

*(Above)* In a subdued living room, a cobalt sofa reads like a bright brushstroke. Styled for Anthropologie.

*(Above)* A color-blocked rug anchors a bedroom vignette. Styled for Beni.

*(Opposite)* Books and objects in a curated spectrum accentuate the terra-cotta-colored carpet and paint of a Manhattan den. Interior design by Studio Giancarlo Valle. Styled for *Architectural Digest*.

FRANCOIS HALARD
BASQUIAT
BAUHAUS
BODY OF ART
JULIE MEHRETU
CHUCK CLOSE
CHARLOTTE PERRIAND
STONE

*(Opposite)* In Brooklyn, a bedside bouquet and the velvet-upholstered bedframe and headboard play off the palette of the painting above. Interior design by Studio Mellone. Styled for *Architectural Digest*.

*(Above)* A rust-colored carpet rivals the New York City skyline in an Upper West Side office. Styled for Studio Mellone.

*(Overleaf)* A shamrock-colored bedspread makes for a verdant landscape in Jonathan Sheffer's Sagaponack bedroom. Interior design by Jack Ceglic. Architecture by Manuel Fernandez-Casteleiro. Styled for *Architectural Digest*.

CLEARTYPE
County-Town
UNITED STATES

When establishing a palette, look for similarities and differences. Is there commonality to celebrate or is there tension to build? How can one element in a room make another shine? The key is to use color very deliberately.



*(Opposite)* Curtains and upholstery in sepia hues riff on a downtown Manhattan loft's terrazzo floor tiles. Interior by Pappas Miron Design. Styled for *Elle Decor*.

If a room is painted, I look for ways to reveal that color—using objects to accentuate it and frame it. Everything else in the room should cater to that color.



*(Opposite)* Sprinkled across a tablescape, marigold blossoms offset the gray and blue tones of the dishes and linens. Styled for Roman and Williams Guild.

# 7

# TACTILE EXPRESSIONS

INVESTIGATING MATERIALITY, TEXTURE,
AND THE SENSUALITY OF SURFACE

Styling is both a visual and a hands-on practice. You may be focused on how a space looks, but in the process you are also immersed in how that space feels, as you arrange and rearrange the objects in a room. And, ultimately, sight and touch should inform one other. The knots on a plank of oak, the grooves on a rock, the crack on a piece of pottery—what excites your fingertips also excites your mind. Surfaces are sentiments of sorts, capable of stirring an emotion or conjuring a memory. I'm usually drawn to nonreflective materials, gravitating toward matte finishes and honed stones. If something is metallic, glazed, or varnished, it should be very intentional. The key, no matter your sensibility, is to be deliberate. Texture can be a unifying theme: a complementary array of ceramic glazes or natural grains or woven textiles. But texture can also be an opportunity for tension and, through that tension, heightened awareness. The smoothness of one object can accentuate the relief of another. Something shiny, juxtaposed with something matte, appears all the more lustrous. And even the slightest imperfection here can cast a halo of perfection there. Through similarities and differences, surfaces project narratives of harmony and conflict. The challenge—and the joy—may be living with both.

COMPOSITE NATURE
MICHELANGELO DRAWINGS

*(Page 183)* Created in collaboration with artist Almine El Gotaibi, a monumental hank of raw wool drapes across my *Spoken Lines* installation in Milan. Styled for Beni.

*(Opposite and Above)* A chorus of fine surfaces, both hard and soft, at the Greenwich Hotel. Interior design by Axel Vervoordt. Styled for Beni.

*(Overleaf)* A patinated expanse offers a nuanced backdrop to a collection of small vessels. Kitchen by Garde Hvalsøe. Architecture by O'Neill Rose Architects. Styled for *Rum*.

*(Opposite)* At a Tribeca apartment, hewn wood in a high-gloss finish offsets elaborate stitchwork. Interior design by Monique Gibson. Architecture by Ike Kligerman Barkley. Styled for *Architectural Digest*.

*(Above)* A tapestry backs a headboard in a downtown Manhattan loft. Interior design by Pappas Miron Design. Styled for *Elle Decor*.

*(Overleaf)* Interior expanses at the Schindler House in West Hollywood create a tripartite framework. Styled for West Elm.

*(Opposite)* The timeworn facade frames a window view of my *Spoken Lines* installation. Styled for Beni.

*(Above)* Weathered woods and textile-bound volumes lend layers to my Tribeca loft.

*(Above)* Expressionistic brushstrokes, sleek finishes, and organic materials in a Tribeca apartment. Styled for Sandra Weingort.

*(Opposite)* Plush pillows add some sybaritic spirit to the same apartment's living room. Styled for Sandra Weingort.

Charlotte Perriand
michelangelo
The Lives of Others
JEAN PROUVÉ
JEAN PROUVÉ
Olivier Dwek
BILLY COTTON
EDWARD WESTON
THE INTERNATIONAL BOOK OF LOFTS
New York Interiors
HOUSE BOOK
EIGHT HOMES · CLEMENTS DESIGN
JACQUES GRANGE
BRUEGEL
FRANK
AMERICAN PAINTING

*(Opposite)* Timber elements abound in my Tribeca loft, where my library and desk reflect a mind at work.

*(Above)* In my dining area, a vintage Pierre Jeanneret cabinet from MDFG bears a hand-carved inscription; the door handle is by Izé.

*(Right)* Shearling upholstery adds a lush moment in my office.

Bring in the vintage and the handmade—things that aren't too precious, that possess patina, that exude history through their wear and tear. Surfaces should tell stories.



*(Opposite)* An immersive tapestry in a Chelsea loft. Interior design by Ryan Lawson. Styled for *Architectural Digest*.

WOLF

*(Opposite)* A custom brass hood and luminous zellige tiles in a Los Angeles house. Interior design by Studio Life/Style. Styled for *California Home+Design*.

*(Above)* Richly figured stone informs the palette of this Tribeca vignette. Interior design by Monique Gibson. Architecture by Ike Kligerman Barkley. Styled for *Architectural Digest*.

*(Above)* The form of one object accentuates the form of the next. Styled for Roman and Williams Guild.

*(Opposite)* A gently draped linen coverlet sets the mood at the Connecticut house of Christian Siriano. Styled for *Architectural Digest*.

*(Overleaf)* Glassware sparkles all the brighter on a crumpled swath of woven fabric. Styled for Roman and Williams Guild.

GENESIS
HENRY MOORE DRAWINGS
THE TOUCH
INTERIORS
In the Studio

Objects have the power to change the atmosphere around them. Search for opportunities to unearth subtlety, complexity, and variety through texture. Reinvigorate what you have through juxtaposition.



*(Opposite)* A variety of different woods becomes a meditation on tone and material. Styled for Roman and Williams Guild.

*(Above)* A newel post reveals the mark of time through imperfections and wear. Styled for Roman and Williams Guild.

*(Opposite)* The grain of a piece of wood, the weave of a textile, the finish of a metallic surface—these small idiosyncrasies add up to something greater. Styled for Sandra Weingort.

Anni Albers On Weaving

Look for differences in texture—pairing something rough with something smooth. There is poetry in friction.



*(Opposite)* Vintage surfaces offer snapshots of humanity at Demisch Danant's *Mises en Scène* exhibition. Styled for Demisch Danant.

# 8

# S I G N S O F L I F E

## FINDING POETRY AND HUMANITY IN EVERYDAY IMPERFECTIONS

Too often, in this shiny Instagram era, we are tyrannized by the prospect of perfection. But flaws are facts of life. Bruises, wrinkles, scratches, spills—the impact of our routines can be found on our bodies and in our spaces. For me, it's been a long journey to accept these messy undertones as I've relinquished the unforgiving ideals of my classical ballet training. But through styling I have discovered the beauty of disarray: the puddle of a drape on the floor, the sensual disorder of a bed, the irregular coil of a lamp cord, even the mundanity of a radiator pipe. These are moments to be savored, not censored. These days, I immediately gravitate toward objects, vignettes, and rooms that foreground humanity, whether an unlit, half-used candle or a door left ajar. The best spaces feel unstudied, the best images voyeuristic. A bookshelf overstuffed with tomes, for example, offers a peek inside a rich imagination, while a sofa imprinted with human forms both suggests and invites repose. (That said, best to pick up your laundry.) And the most poignant surfaces are those that have evolved with time, like marble stained with rings or brass clouded with patina. When people say that a space feels cold it's usually because everything is too polished, too new, too neat. There's always the temptation to hide the realness—but the realness is the charm. Pause before adjusting it.

*(Page 215)* A table set for an alfresco feast. Styled for Roman and Williams Guild.

*(Opposite)* Movement in the form of curtains not fully drawn. Styled for Anna Karlin.

*(Above)* Plates, piled high, and an abundance of lemons anticipate a celebration. Styled for Roman and Williams Guild.

The best rooms look like someone was just there. That can come from an open book, a pillow that's been tossed aside, or an object that's slightly askew. On set and at home, I am forever chasing that unstyled feeling.

*(Above)* An extinguished flame's tendrils of smoke. Styled for Roman and Williams Guild.

*(Opposite)* A tasseled throw blanket, draped just so. Styled for Zara Home.

*(Overleaf)* A bathrobe thrown over the edge of the tub, a body in absentia. Styled for Zara Home.

*(Opposite)* Scored cutting boards in a corner of Kirsten Dunst's Los Angeles kitchen. Interior design by Hallworth. Styled for *Architectural Digest*.

*(Above)* The everyday ritual of breaking bread. Styled for West Elm.

*(Above)* Samples crowd into a corner of my Tribeca office.

*(Opposite)* A peaceful shower space. Styled for Zara Home.

Books convey a sense of lived-in authenticity that gives a sense of grounded reality to a space. I love pairing books with other unique finds or using them as a pedestal. Stack them high enough and you'll have a chic side table.



*(Opposite)* At the Sagaponack house of Jonathan Sheffer, a salon-style arrangement of art—some hung, some propped—and a table set for chess reveal a mind's many fascinations. Interior design by Jack Ceglic. Architecture by Manuel Fernandez-Casteleiro. Styled for *Architectural Digest*.

*(Above)* An open window at my Tribeca loft lets the sounds of the city inside.

*(Opposite)* At a historic house in Marfa, the entry's double doors open to a pedestal table and a Richard Serra artwork beyond, beckoning visitors. Interior design by Jeffrey Bilhuber and Madison Cox. Architecture by Selldorf Architects. Styled for *Architectural Digest*.

*(Opposite)* Water poured and salad served at a table set for two. Styled for Zara Home.

*(Above)* Meal prep underway. Styled for Zara Home.

There's nothing quite as warm as a table just after a meal—chairs staggered, linens thrown, flatware scattered.



*(Opposite)* Stacked books reflect accumulated knowledge in my Brooklyn Heights apartment. Styled for *T* magazine.

A History of Interior Design
A Visual Inventory
John Pawson
THE KINFOLK HOME
CALDERONE
LIVE BEAUTIFUL
noguchi
JOSEPH DIRAND Interior
Houses | Atelier AM
e Art of Richard Diebenkorn
domus
domus
TASCHEN
INTERIOR DESIGN AND DEC
Ellen DeGeneres Home
TERENCE CONRAN'S HOUSE BOOK
BECOMING by CINDY CRAWFORD
Building Beauty The Alchemy of Design
JACK
robert Rauschenberg combines
Monet
FRANCOIS HALARD

*(Above)* An overstuffed Marfa library captures the imagination. Interior design by Jeffrey Bilhuber and Madison Cox. Architecture by Selldorf Architects. Styled for *Architectural Digest*.

ARCHITECTURE
GILBERT & GEORGE
WARHOL
GORDON PARKS I AM YOU
de Kooning
BILL VIOLA
ANDY WARHOL
ROTHKO

*(Opposite)* Logs burn in a historic hearth, warming the room and the atmosphere. Styled for Roman and Williams Guild.

*(Above)* Persimmon branches piled on the coffee table hint at a world of wild things. Styled for Roman and Williams Guild.

# *Acknowledgments*

This book is a meditation on objects but it is also a love letter to people—my many champions, collaborators, and kindred creative spirits. The images would not be possible were it not for the photographers—in particular, Adrian Gaut, Rich Stapleton, Stephen Kent Johnson, and William Jess Laird, who have generously allowed me to share their vision. I'm so grateful. Endless thanks as well to all the designers who have trusted me to represent their work, especially Robin Standefer and Stephen Alesch, Giancarlo Valle, Andre Mellone, Ryan Lawson, Monique Gibson, Jack Ceglic, and Sandra Weingort. Bearing witness to your process has been a master class. To the brands and galleries with whom I have partnered—Beni, Demisch Danant, Anna Karlin, Menu, Zara Home, Anthropologie, West Elm, Crate & Barrel—it's been an honor to arrange your things. And to the magazines such as *T* and *Architectural Digest* that have helped guide my career, I am humbled by your confidence in my ability to communicate your stories. I could not have created this book without the expert guidance of my editorial partners: literary agent Carla Glasser, graphic designer Javas Lehn, writer Sam Cochran, and Rizzoli's Charles Miers and Philip Reeser. You're my dream team. And I could not have even become a stylist were it not for the encouragement of my agents Rob Magnotta and Kacy Karp, or the help of every single person on set along the way. Finally, I would like to give special thanks to my dear friends Athena Calderone, David Alhadeff, Tom Delavan, Dobrinka Salzman, and Robert Wright for their constant support; and to my family, especially my twin brother, Caleb, who taught me the meaning of home. You are all the best things in my life.

COLIN KING



*(Opposite)* In my Tribeca bedroom, my vases for Menu amid stacks of books.

JUDD
FONTANA ON THE THRESHOLD
MORGAN FALCONER
PAINTING BEYOND POLLOCK
POLLOCK
CHINATI
A FRAME FOR
ESSENTIAL EAMES
THE DAYBOOKS OF EDW

First published in the
United States of America in 2023 by
Rizzoli International Publications, Inc.
300 Park Avenue South
New York, New York 10010
rizzoliusa.com

Publisher: Charles Miers
Senior Editor: Philip Reeser
Production Manager: Alyn Evans
Design Coordinator: Olivia Russin
Copy Editor: Victoria Brown
Proofreader: Sarah Stump
Managing Editor: Lynn Scrabis

Book Design: Javas Lehn Studio


Text by Colin King with Sam Cochran

Milton Resnick painting on front of jacket:
Courtesy the Milton Resnick and Pat Passlof
Foundation and Cheim & Read, New York



ISBN: 978-0-8478-9910-4
Library of Congress Control Number: 2022941768

2023 2024 2025 / 10 9 8 7 6 5 4
Printed in China

Photography Credits:

Rich Stapleton: 2, 5, 8, 12, 17, 22, 28, 32–33, 47–49, 55, 59, 77, 88–89, 103, 106–7, 220–1, 225, 228, 239

Gentl and Hyers: 6, 206, 208, 218

Adrian Gaut: 18–21, 24, 29–31, 34–35, 45, 53, 60, 62–64, 66–67, 69, 72, 78–79, 81, 84–85, 90–93, 96–97, 105, 110–3, 115, 122, 128–31, 136–7, 140–8, 155–8, 168–9, 178, 185, 186–7, 190–1, 193–7, 202, 204–5, 209–10, 215–7, 223–4, 236–7

Joaquin Laguinge: 25, 167

Andrew Jacobs: 26–27, 120–1

Nicole Franzen: 36, 233

William Abranowicz: 37, 68, 188, 201

Yago Castromil: 38, 98, 117 (top left), 132

Stephen Kent Johnson: 39, 41, 46, 52, 57, 159–62, 166, 170–2, 177, 184, 189, 199

William Jess Laird: 50–51, 65, 82, 119, 134–5, 153, 173, 229, 234–5

Colin King: 56, 61, 86–87, 104, 108–9, 116, 117 (bottom right), 118, 133, 138–9, 203

Blaine Davis: 70–71

Frederik Vercruysse: 80, 219, 230–1

Kovi Konowiecki: 83, 95

Pippa Drummond: 127

Philip Messmann: 154

Victoria Hely-Hutchinson: 163–5

Tim Williams: 174–5, 226

Sean Davidson: 183, 192

Sam Frost: 200

Laure Joliet: 222